I0490399

C.B. VELA

# Selling As An Introvert

*5 Ways to Succeed in Sales as an Introvert*

Copyright © 2023 by C.B. Vela

All rights reserved. No part of this publication may be reproduced, stored or transmitted in any form or by any means, electronic, mechanical, photocopying, recording, scanning, or otherwise without written permission from the publisher. It is illegal to copy this book, post it to a website, or distribute it by any other means without permission.

C.B. Vela asserts the moral right to be identified as the author of this work.

C.B. Vela has no responsibility for the persistence or accuracy of URLs for external or third-party Internet Websites referred to in this publication and does not guarantee that any content on such Websites is, or will remain, accurate or appropriate.

Designations used by companies to distinguish their products are often claimed as trademarks. All brand names and product names used in this book and on its cover are trade names, service marks, trademarks and registered trademarks of their respective owners. The publishers and the book are not associated with any product or vendor mentioned in this book. None of the companies referenced within the book have endorsed the book.

First edition

This book was professionally typeset on Reedsy.
Find out more at reedsy.com

"Contrary to all myths and beliefs, introverts make the best salespeople."

Mathew Pollard

# Contents

# 1

# Introduction

Are you an introvert looking to succeed in sales? You may think that extroverts have the upper hand in this industry, but that couldn't be further from the truth. With the right strategies, introverts can excel in sales just as much as their more outgoing counterparts. In this book, you'll learn a little bit about me, we'll explore what it means to be an introvert, we'll explore five proven ways introverts can tap into their strengths, overcome common challenges, and achieve success in sales.

# 2

# A Little Bit About Me

I have been in sales for 15 years and if you were to tell anybody from my childhood that I would one day be a Vice President of Sales for an international software company, they would say you were lying. Let me tell you why, I grew up in South Side Chicago and was an elect mute until I was in 4th grade. This basically meant that I didn't speak to a single soul in school. Not to teachers or classmates. I had one friend who I would whisper to in the cafeteria and she would let other people know what I wanted. My mother would have to record me reading on a cassette player in order to receive an oral reading grade at school. So to say that I was an introvert, would be an understatement. I struggled throughout my whole childhood and into college with my introversion not really knowing why I was the way I was and why I felt the way I did around others. I also never understood why it was so difficult for me to be social. It wasn't until I took a class in communications in college and heard the word "introverts" that everything started to make sense to me. The more I understood introversion, the more I sought ways to work around my personality type to reach for my goals and dreams, especially when I set my sights on sales.

I didn't start off with sights on sales right out of college. I was always told by counselors in school that because of my personality, my best options would be to seek a career that would allow me to work on my own. Things like an accountant, writer, data analyst, etc. What I didn't hear was the one I really wanted to get into, business. None of the careers they suggested interested me, so I went with my mother's advice and chose education. Scared me to death when I had to face 22, 2nd graders in my first class. The only words that I kept repeating to myself were those my mother would tell me. "Why are you afraid? Do they know more about what you will teach them than you?" Obviously I knew the answer, so I pushed through everyday until I gained enough confidence to do it again the following year and 6 years after. Funny thing about life is how your steps lead you to paths you never imagined were available to you. Thanks to people who saw strengths in me that I didn't see myself, I was encouraged to pursue leadership. Although I was afraid, I knew that I wanted to seek advancement in my career, so I pushed through my doubts and fears and moved into an assistant principal position and eventually ended my career in education as an elementary school principal. Loved every moment of it until my husband had a career opportunity that moved us across the state to a new community. It was at this crossroad in my life that I felt it was time to pursue a dream that I always had, a career in business or more specifically - sales. Now you may be thinking that my leadership opportunities allowed me to learn how to be successful in sales, little did I know the road ahead was going to have a rough start, but this path would lead me to the best path and career that I could have ever dreamed of. Life was about to get exciting and can't wait to share it with you!

# 3

# Definition of Introversion

Before I get into the meat of my book, I want to spend some time discussing introversion. So what does it mean to be an introvert? According to Webster dictionary, an introvert is a person whose personality is characterized by introversion : a typically reserved or quiet person who tends to be introspective and enjoys spending time alone. More specifically, Introversion is a personality trait characterized by a focus on internal feelings, thoughts, and experiences rather than on external stimulation and social interaction. Introverts tend to prefer solitary activities, enjoy spending time alone, and find social situations draining. They tend to be more introspective and reflective, and they process information internally before responding. This trait is one aspect of a person's personality and is not necessarily a problem or weakness, but rather a natural variation in how people experience and interact with the world. After I discovered this as being my personality trait, I was better prepared to tackle my world. This is my hope for you as you read this book. If you resonate with any part of the introversion definition and you have chosen to pursue the world of sales like I did, let's look introversion in the eye and use this trait as our secret weapon.

# 4

# Personality Challenges Faced by Introverts in Sales

Now when I started to pursue sales as a career, I faced several challenges even before applying for a sales job. Interview after interview, I would hear some prerequisites that I wasn't sure my personality was prepared to do. One of which was **comfort with social interactions**. I always felt drained by constant social interactions and most sales jobs descriptions would require attending network events and being in social settings. How was I going to get myself mentally prepared for these types of events? I was also challenged by my **preference for solitude**. I would always prefer to work alone and in many sales interviews, sales people work in a team environment. Would I be a good team player? Another job description detail that I struggled with was to create strong rapport with clients. I always had **difficulty with small talk**. I struggled with ways to strike a conversation with complete strangers. Would this make it difficult for me to build rapport with clients? Once I started thinking about small talk, I also thought about presenting in front of large crowds. Since I was also shy, I was also challenged with how to **overcome shyness**: I always had difficulty speaking up and expressing my ideas in front of a group. Would I be able to do this? You have probably caught on that introverts also overthink. This comes from one of the biggest challenges of them all, *fear of rejection*. I had so much fear pursuing a sales position that just the thought of being rejected felt overwhelming. This really comes from introverts being more sensitive to rejection than others. So the biggest question in my mind was will I struggle with the constant rejection that is part of sales?

Have these personality challenges come up for you in your pursuit of sales positions? If they have, don't worry, the good news is that our personality type actually makes for a better salesperson than an extrovert personality. In the next chapters, I will share the ways I overcame the challenges I mentioned along with the mindset I brought to the table to not only help make me successful at sales, but made me a top salesperson in my company with opportunity after opportunity for career advancement. Trust me, if I can find success in sales, so can YOU!

# 5

# Importance of Embracing your Personality Type

B efore I start talking about ways that I overcame the challenges I faced in my pursuit of a sales position, it's important for you to understand that we need to embrace our personality type because it's the only way we will believe that we can be successful at sales.

So as introverts, what are some traits that makeup our personality type? Here are some that can be important in sales:

1. Introspection: Introverts tend to spend a lot of time thinking and reflecting on their thoughts, feelings, and experiences, so it's especially important to understand this trait and how you will use it to your advantage in sales.
2. Solitude: Introverts enjoy spending time alone and find it rejuvenating. Although this may be counter intuitive in sales, it will become important to understand as we navigate our day to day in sales.
3. Low stimulation tolerance: Introverts can quickly become overwhelmed by high-stimulation environments, such as loud, busy

public spaces. This is important to understand so we can understand when we reach our tolerance threshold.

4. Small talk aversion: Introverts may feel uncomfortable making small talk and prefer more meaningful conversations. This is important to understand in sales and will be spending some time talking about overcoming this aversion in a future chapter.

5. Observant: Introverts are often very observant and perceptive, paying attention to details and picking up on nonverbal cues. This is going to be one of our secret weapons as we navigate sales opportunities.

6. Reflective: Introverts are often reflective and introspective, taking the time to consider their thoughts and feelings before acting. This is another secret weapon that will help us understand customers.

7. Listening skills: Introverts are often excellent listeners, paying close attention to others and responding thoughtfully. Out of all our traits, this is the most important one. This trait is by far our best weapon that others in sales tend to lack.

It's important to remember that everyone is unique and may exhibit different combinations of these traits. Additionally, some experts believe that introversion is a spectrum, and some people may be more introverted than others. Whichever trait you exhibit, how will embracing these traits to help you in sales?

Here are some important points on why it's important to embrace your personality type.

1. Improved self-awareness: Understanding your personality trait helps you better understand your strengths, weaknesses, and how you react to different situations.

2. Increased confidence: Embracing your personality trait can boost

your self-esteem and increase your confidence in your abilities.

3. Better relationships: Accepting your personality trait can improve your relationships with others, as you will be able to communicate more effectively and understand their perspectives.

4. Improved decision-making: Understanding your personality trait can help you make more informed decisions about your career, hobbies, and personal life.

5. Better work-life balance: Embracing your personality trait can help you find a better work-life balance by pursuing activities and careers that align with your natural tendencies.

Overall, embracing your personality trait can lead to a more fulfilling life, improved well-being and success in sales. Now let's dig into some techniques I used to overcome the challenges I faced and how I embraced my personality to find success in sales.

# 6

# 5 Ways to Succeed

**O**vercome Challenges

Now let's dig into the steps you can take to overcome challenges you will encounter as an introvert in sales. The ones I will cover here include the 5 challenges I faced when starting in sales. 1) Comfortable in social interactions 2) Preference for solitude 3) Difficulty with small talk 4) Overcoming shyness and 5) Fear of rejection.

Comfortable with Social Interactions

The first challenge I mentioned I encountered when looking for opportunities in sales was how to become comfortable *with social interactions.* These are the steps I took to feel comfortable in social settings. This didn't happen overnight, but the more I did the following, the more comfortable I felt in social settings. Use these strategies and you too can become comfortable with social interactions.

1. Practice: Social interactions can become more comfortable with practice, so start by gradually exposing yourself to more social

situations.

2. Preparation: Prepare for the event, this can help reduce your anxiety in social interactions. Always research the topic they are discussing, plan what you want to say, and mentally rehearse the conversation.

3. Focus on others: Focusing on the other person and their interests will help you feel more relaxed in social situations.

4. Set boundaries: Always set a time limit for your interactions. Setting boundaries to recharge after social interactions will always help you avoid becoming overwhelmed.

5. Find like-minded people: If you have to attend an event, always seek out groups or events where you can connect with others who share similar interests, reducing the pressure to socialize.

6. Leverage technology: Always leverage technology to communicate and connect with others prior to an event, such as through email, messaging, or videoconferencing.

Remember, everyone is unique and may find other strategies that work best for them. It's important for us to experiment with different methods and find what works best for you in overcoming social interactions. The key is to stick with what works and be consistent in using them.

Preference for Solitude

Another question I faced when interviewing was whether I would be able to work in a team environment when I preferred working alone. When I transitioned to working in sales, I discovered ways to embrace a team environment while staying true to myself. Here are some ways you can work in a team environment and provide yourself the solitude you need:

1. Schedule alone time: Always schedule alone time during your day to

recharge and maintain your energy levels, while still being available for team collaboration.

2. Communicate needs: communication is key, so always voice your need for solitude to the team and negotiate a flexible schedule that accommodates this preference. Team members will always be willing to accommodate this need.

3. Leverage technology: Leverage technology as much as possible to participate in team meetings and discussions, such as through videoconferencing or instant messaging.

4. Find a supportive team: Always look for a team that values individual differences and encourages all members to work in their preferred style.

5. Contribute in your own way: Contribute to the team by taking on tasks that allow you to work independently and utilize your strengths.

6. Be an active listener: Actively listen and participate in team discussions, offer your insights and ideas, and build relationships with your colleagues.

Remember, teams are made up of individuals with different personality traits, and it's important for us to find a way to work effectively with the team while also staying true to your natural tendencies.

Small Talk with Strangers

Another challenge that I faced in sales was how to make small talk with strangers. The thought of having to talk to strangers and what to ask made me anxious. I managed through that and you can too. Here are some tips I used to overcome this challenge and some I challenge you to try to make small talk with strangers:

1. Prepare beforehand: Prepare for small talk by thinking about topics that interest them and questions you would like to ask.
2. Find common ground: Look for common ground with the other person, such as shared interests, hobbies, or experiences.
3. Ask open-ended questions: Start a conversation by asking open-ended questions that encourage the other person to talk and share more about themselves.
4. Listen actively: Practice active listening by paying attention to what the other person is saying, asking follow-up questions, and showing interest in their conversation.
5. Be yourself: Be yourself and avoid trying to pretend to be someone you're not, which can lead to increased comfort and more meaningful conversations.
6. Take breaks: Take breaks when you need to recharge, and then rejoin the conversation when you feel ready.

Remember, small talk is a skill that can be improved with practice. By focusing on the other person and their interests, you can make small talk more enjoyable and build deeper connections with others.

Overcoming Shyness

This challenge was probably my most difficult one to overcome. Not all introverts are shy, but this was one of my traits and having the spotlight was not fun for me. I knew that the only way I could be successful in sales was if I was a good presenter and would not be afraid to present to large groups of people. I couldn't do that if I let my shyness get in the way, so I worked hard at setting a positive mindset and practiced certain things to help me through any presentation or conversion with large groups of people.. If shyness is part of your personality traits. Practice these tips and you too can embrace your shyness with success.

1. Practice self-affirmations: Encourage yourself by reminding yourself of your strengths, skills, and accomplishments, and focus on positive thoughts.
2. Prepare: Preparation can help reduce the anxiety and stress that can come with a large group presentation, take some time to research the people you'll be presenting to, or think about topics you can bring up in conversation.
3. Focus on others: When in presentation situations, focus on others and try to get to know them. Ask questions and listen as you present to what they have to say, and try to find common interests along the way.
4. Participate in small steps: Take small steps towards overcoming shyness by participating in social activities prior to the large gathering/presentation, so that you feel comfortable with the situation. Gradually increase your comfort level by trying new things or approaches to your presentations.
5. Seek support: Surround yourself with supportive friends and family members who encourage and motivate you. Seek out a mentor or coach who can help you build confidence and overcome shyness.
6. Get involved in activities you enjoy: Participating in activities you enjoy can boost your confidence and help you meet new people.
7. Accept your introversion: It's important to embrace your introversion and accept that it's a part of who you are. Understanding and accepting your introversion can help you feel more comfortable and confident in any presentation or social situations.

Remember, overcoming shyness takes time and practice. It's important to be patient with yourself and focus on taking small steps towards your goal. With persistence and determination, you can overcome shyness and build the confidence you need to succeed in any presentation or social situation.

Fear of Rejection

I believe that above all challenges I had with sales as my career, by far the most overarching challenge was fear of rejection. I spent more time on this challenge during my first year of sales than any other challenge I faced and I believe 99% of all introverts that give up on sales is because of the challenge with fear. I worked hard at developing some tactics that would help me through this fear and I believe these tactics can help you as well. Here are the tactics I recommend you use to overcome fear of rejection:

1. Practice self-compassion: Practice self-compassion and remind yourself that rejection is a normal part of life and doesn't define their worth as a person. Do this over and over. It does get easier with practice.
2. Re-frame rejection: Re-frame rejection as feedback, and view it as an opportunity to learn and grow. Don't think of a 'no' as something final, think of it as a 'maybe' or a next time.
3. Focus on your strengths: Focus on your strengths and the things that you bring to the table, which can help boost your confidence and reduce the fear of rejection.
4. Take calculated risks: Take calculated risks and put yourself out there, even if it means facing the possibility of rejection. Over time, the fear of rejection will become less intense as you will become more confident and comfortable with the process.
5. Seek support: Seek support from friends, family who can offer encouragement and help you overcome your fear of rejection.
6. Celebrate small victories: Celebrate your small victories regardless of how small it is and acknowledge your progress, which can help boost your confidence and reduce your fear of rejection.

Remember, everyone experiences fear of rejection at some point in their lives, but it's possible to overcome it with persistence and effort. By focusing on their strengths, taking calculated risks, and seeking support, you can work through your fear and become more confident in yourself.

This sums up how I overcame my initial challenges with sales, but it doesn't stop here. My success hindered on other things that I needed to put in place in order for me to be successful in sales. In the following chapters, I will take a deeper dive in some of the additional ways I prepared myself for my career in sales. My hope is that these additional ways will also prepare you for a successful career in sales.

# 7

# Preparation and Planning

O nce we identify and work toward facing our challenges, we also have to take into consideration other things we need to do to prepare and plan for our career in sales. The first one is preparing and planning for sales meetings. I touched earlier on how one of the personality traits we can have is shyness and how that can affect our ability to present and interact in large meetings. Uncovering this challenge is important and working toward pushing through the shyness is our ultimate goal, but prior to this, we also need to learn how to prepare and plan for the sales meeting. If we can do a good job of preparing ourselves, this can also play a significant role in helping us push through our shyness. Here are some ways that I prepare and plan for sales meetings and ways that you can incorporate in your preparation as well:

1. Research the prospect: Research the prospect and gather informa-tion about their company, industry, and specific needs, which can help you tailor your approach and increase your chances of success.
2. Develop a script: Develop a script or outline of the key points you want to cover during the meeting, which can help you stay focused

and ensure that you cover all the important information.

3. Visualize success: Visualize the meeting going well and imagine yourself successfully connecting with the prospect, which can help build your confidence and reduce your nerves.

4. Find allies: Seek out allies, such as a more extroverted colleague, who can help introduce you to the prospect and provide support during the meeting.

5. Ask for feedback: Ask for feedback from trusted colleagues or friends, who can offer constructive criticism and help you refine your approach.

6. Take breaks: Plan for breaks between meetings to recharge and maintain your energy levels, which can help you perform at your best.

Remember, preparation and planning are key to success in sales meetings, especially for us as introverts. By doing the research, developing a script, and seeking support from allies, we can increase our chances of success and build stronger relationships with our prospects.

# 8

## Rehearsing Sales Pitches

I f all you take is just this one way of achieving success in sales, I hope it's this way - rehearsing sales pitches. I can't tell you how beneficial this was for me in the beginning. It can be daunting to your personality to go head first into a meeting without prepping. It's hard enough to prepare yourself mentally for the challenge, so the best way to help yourself is to rehearse, rehearse, rehearse. It will be time consuming at first, but it will pay off and you will need to do it less and less as your confidence and knowledge increases. So here are some ways I prepared and ways that you can do the same:

1. Practice with a trusted friend or colleague: Practice your sales pitch with a trusted friend or colleague who can provide feedback and help you refine your approach.
2. Record and review: Record yourself practicing your sales pitch and then review it to identify areas for improvement. This was my most favorite and rewarding.
3. Use visualization techniques: Use visualization techniques, such as imagining yourself giving the sales pitch in front of an audience, to build your confidence and reduce their nerves. I know it sounds

SELLING AS AN INTROVERT

weird, but trust me, it works.

4. Role-play: Role-play with a colleague or friend, simulating a real sales pitch, which can help you become more comfortable and confident with the process. It's tough at first, but does get easier and really pays off.

5. Take breaks: Take breaks between rehearsals to recharge and maintain your energy levels, which can help you perform at your best.

6. Focus on the prospect: Focus on the needs and interests of the prospect, rather than on your own nerves, which can help you connect more effectively and build stronger relationships.

Remember, rehearsing is a critical part of preparing for a sales pitch. By practicing with a trusted friend or colleague, recording and reviewing your performance, and using visualization techniques, you can increase your chances of success and build your confidence.

# 9

# Staying Motivated

The toughest roadblock you will have to overcome in sales is staying motivated. Sales often feels like a roller coaster. As introverts, these challenges can be overwhelming and giving up might appear to be the best decision to make, but it wouldn't be. Sales is one of the most lucrative careers out there and our limit to how much we can earn is really capped by the limitations we set for ourselves. Anybody can be good at sales, regardless of our personality. If thoughts of giving up creep up, here are some ways that you can remain motivated:

1. Set achievable goals: Set achievable goals for yourself and track your progress, which can provide a sense of accomplishment and keep you motivated.
2. Celebrate success: Remind yourself to celebrate your successes, no matter how small, which can help build your confidence and maintain your motivation.
3. Focus on the impact: Focus on the impact that your sales efforts are having on your prospects, which can help you see the value in what you are doing and maintain your motivation.
4. Take breaks: Don't forget to take breaks to recharge and maintain

your energy levels, which can help you perform at your best and stay motivated.

5. Surround themselves with supportive people: Always remember to surround yourself with supportive people, such as colleagues, friends, or family, who can provide encouragement and help you maintain your motivation.
6. Reflect on your values: Reflect on your values and what you stand for, which can help you find meaning and purpose in your work and maintain your motivation.

Remember, motivation is key to success in sales. By setting achievable goals, celebrating success, and surrounding yourself with supportive people, you can maintain your motivation and achieve success.

# 10

# Adapting your Sales Style to your Personality

I believe that being an introvert is a gift for sales and I wouldn't change my personality with any other. People ask me how I have achieved tremendous success in sales knowing my personality and challenges I face everyday. My response is because I learned to embrace and adapt my sales style to my personality. If you learn to do the same, you too can achieve tremendous success in sales. If you are looking for ways to do this, here are some ways that I adapted my sales style to my personality. I am confident you can achieve the same following these ideas:

1. Focus on one-on-one interactions: Look for one-on-one interactions with prospects, where you can build deeper connections and engage in more meaningful conversations.
2. Prepare thoroughly: Always remember to prepare thoroughly for each sales interaction, researching the prospect, developing a script, and anticipating questions, which can help you feel more confident and in control.
3. Listen actively: Our strength is to listen, so listen actively to your prospects and pay attention to their needs, which can help build

rapport and establish trust.

4. Emphasize the value proposition: You bring great value to a prospect, so emphasize the value proposition of your products or services, and articulate the benefits to the prospect, which can help build interest and drive results.

5. Use technology to your advantage: Technology is our best friend, so leverage technology, such as email, video conferencing, and online presentations, to reach out to prospects and build relationships, which can help you avoid the stress and anxiety that can come with face-to-face interactions.

6. Partner with extroverts: Extroverts can be a good resource, so partner with extroverted colleagues who can help you reach out to prospects, generate leads, and build relationships, which can help you achieve your desired outcomes.

Remember, sales success is not dependent on being an extrovert. By focusing on one-on-one interactions, preparing thoroughly, and leveraging technology, we can adapt our sales style to our personality and achieve our desired outcomes.

# 11

# Conclusion

I n conclusion, I hope this book has given you some evidence that introverts have unique strengths and qualities that can be leveraged for success in sales. By understanding introversion and the challenges faced by introverts in sales, we can start embracing our personality type and succeed by overcoming these challenges. We can over achieve by preparing and planning for sales meetings. We can also rehearse sales pitches and most importantly make sure we are staying focused and motivated. Our unique personality can be so well adapted to sales that once we get our first taste of success, we will never picture ourselves doing anything else.

I want to leave you with some words of encouragement that helped me take a leap of faith into the most challenging and rewarding career for introverts - sales.

❤ Remember that Introversion is a valuable trait that sets you apart and brings unique strengths to the table.

❤ Your attention to detail, thoughtfulness, and listening skills are important qualities that can help you connect with prospects and build lasting relationships.

❤ Your ability to think deeply and reflect on your experiences can help you develop a more strategic and effective sales approach.

❤ Embrace your introversion and use it to your advantage.

❤ Your quiet confidence and focus can help you stand out and make a positive impact.

❤ There is no one right way to approach sales.

❤ Your introversion can be an asset, helping you build deeper connections with prospects and deliver valuable insights.

❤ Don't be afraid to be yourself. Your authentic and genuine approach will resonate with prospects and help you build trust.

Lastly, always remember that it's important for us as introverts to embrace our strengths and use them to our advantage. By focusing on our unique qualities and approaching sales in a way that works best for us, we can achieve our desired outcomes and make a positive impact in our careers and the world around us.

Wishing you tremendous success in sales. You can do this, rooting for you!

www.ingramcontent.com/pod-product-compliance
Lightning Source LLC
Chambersburg PA
CBHW070319240526
45467CB00046B/2059